THE MAP

Numbers indicate chapter page numbers.

MICHIGAN BACK ROADS

4

By Ron Rademacher

No part of this book may be reproduced or transmitted in any form or by any means, electronic or mechanical, including photocopying, recording, or by any informational storage or retrieval system, except by a reviewer who may quote brief passages in a review to be printed in a magazine or newspaper without permission in writing from the publisher.

First Edition

Back Roads Publications

Bellevue, Michigan 49021

Copyright © 2012. All Rights Reserved

TABLE OF CONTENTS

Alden's Mill House	9
Dowling General Store	13
Good Hart General Store	19
Gorgeous Gardens	23
Harbor Light Gallery	27
Last Original Tourist Trap	31
Lavender Labyrinth	37
Magic Capital of the World	41
Moosetales	45
Mystery in Ontonagon	49
Port Oneida	53
Purple Pear	57
Shrine of the Pines	61
Storybook Village	65
Tasty Nut Shop	69
Ten Mile Creek Forge	73
Tomb of the Cow	77
Treasure in Capac	81
Treasure in Manton	85
Two Shops and a Ghost	89

AKNOWLEDGEMENTS

Thanks again to the shops who offer these books to their customers, to the organizations who invite me to tell these stories in my shows, and to my proofreader, Terry, who makes it possible to finally finish.

The content of this book is the opinion of the author and does not constitute legal or travel advice.

This book is dedicated to the memory of Richard Guy Jarvis. He loved the back roads, the stories from the past, and the legends as much as I do.

ALDEN'S MILL HOUSE

The Shop:

The Mill House in Alden is so great, that we rarely travel into the northwest region of Michigan without making a point to stop there. In 1984 Eugene Moglovkin, known as Chef Gino, developed his signature all purpose seasoning, "Miracle Blend" as well as other Pepper Mill Spices.

Today the shop offers dozens and dozens of seasonings and spices unlike any other shop. Not only do they manufacture the tastiest spices you will find, this is a shop that men can enjoy as well. I don't know many guys who don't spend time at the barbeque grill. Alden's Mill House has the spices and kitchen essentials that the guys are looking for.

What You'll Find:

The Alden Mill House is located on Helena in downtown Alden, Michigan about three blocks from the boat ramp on beautiful Torch Lake. To get to the entrance you wander through custom gardens that are filled with exotic plantings,

whimsical sculptures and shaded sitting areas. Inside, the store is a riot of variety, a cornucopia of seasonings. Most are ground and mixed on the premises and each bottle is hand-packed. A few are not to be missed such as, the pure ground garlic, Hungarian paprika and the Malabar Island Pepper. A panic breaks out in our kitchen when we run out of any of these.
There are simply too many delicious spices to describe and some of the custom blends are completely unique.

In addition, the shop offers an endless variety of utensils and culinary tools. Plan a little extra time, you can easily lose track while inside this remarkable shop. Oh, don't forget the kosher flake salt. With no iodine it is very tasty and excellent for preparing a brine.

Directions:

Alden is on Torch Lake about 1/2 hour north of Kalkaska and 10 minutes from Bellaire.

Side Trips:

About 10 minutes away is the entertaining town of Bellaire. Great shops line the main street and there are unusual places to visit. Lulu's Bistro offers an amazing menu, everything there is delicious. The Bellaire Smokehouse produces the most delicious white fish pate' I have found. The Bellaire Bed & Breakfast sets a table that delights everyone who stays there.

A bit further north on Route 66 is the community of Ironton. It may be small but it is home to the Ironton Ferry. This may be the shortest ferry ride you will ever take. The whole thing lasts about 2 minutes and the ferry only holds about 4 cars at a time. It is great fun just the same.

A bit south and just north of Kingsley is Mayfield Pond. Outdoorsmen will recognize it as the birthplace of the Adam's Fly, the most successful fishing fly ever developed. An original is on display in the library in downtown Kingsley.

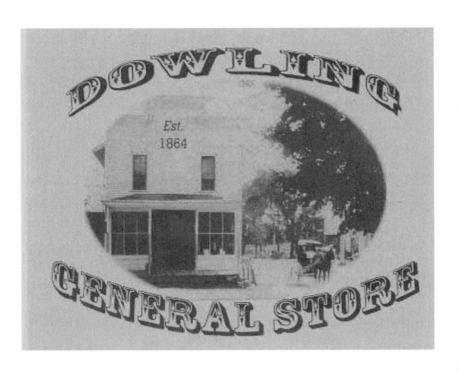

DOWLING GENERAL STORE

The Trip:

A relaxing drive through the rolling hills of south central Michigan can sometimes result in a step back in time. That is exactly what happens if you come across the Dowling General Store. Except for the addition of electricity and refrigeration, the Dowling General Store is very much like it was when it was established in 1864. The exterior is still white clapboard with large windows facing the main road and the ornate facade topping off the front of second story.

This is an old country store and they try to use locally grown ingredients for the wonderful baked goods they make. It is very likely that you will see Amish horse and buggy rigs parked here while the farmers deliver produce.

What You'll Find:

The first thing you will notice is the fantastic aroma that fills the air. Bruce and Sandy are famous in these parts for the mouth-watering baked goods they offer up every day. Donuts and cookies are the favorites. I can tell you that a simple cinnamon donut here, fresh from the oven of course, is a taste delight to be savored. The only problem is that you may eat them all on the way before you can get home. Once you get over the first impact of the delicious smells you can enjoy the atmosphere. Baked goods in glass cases, old, old hardwood floors, home-made ice cream and a couple of simple tables.

You can linger for conversation and a game of checkers or just wander around and admire all of the antiques and artifacts from by gone days. There are a few dry goods available. Some fishing gear if you are headed for one of the nearby lakes, and fish stories in case you don't have one of your own.

The Ghost and The Tunnel:

There are great stories from the history of the store. The owners can give you details. The Dowling General Store has served as a gathering place for the locals and as a refreshing pause for travelers since it was built. Back in the day, the second floor served as a dance hall, among other things, and was a big hit on Saturday nights. The second story of the store is closed at this time but, that doesn't mean it is unoccupied. For many years there have been encounters with "Howard" the ghost. Some say he used to live up there and some say he never missed a chance to cut a rug at the Saturday night hoedowns. It doesn't matter which story you go with. People from all over keep running into Howard. Sometimes he is in the store and sometimes he is outside. Sometimes there is just the sound of someone dancing away late at night in the old dance hall upstairs.

Another story, based on historical fact, is about the old tunnel. It seems that some years ago, the hardwood floors on the main level were buckling and had generally become less level. Folks decided to check the foundations in the basement and during that inspection discovered alcoves hidden behind the walls. Further investigations revealed that, at one time, The Dowling General Store was an important stop on the "Underground Railroad". The alcoves were secret places where refugees could hide and rest.

There is more. While looking into the foundation issues, they also discovered the location of the old tunnel that used to lead under the road to a house on the other side. It is said that a doctor owned that house and when travelers on the underground railroad needed medical attention, the doctor could make his way through the tunnel, treat those in need and return to his home without anyone being able to detect the hiding places under the store.

Directions:

Dowling is about 15 minutes north of Battle Creek, Michigan on Route 37. The store is at the junction of 37 and the Dowling Rd. They are open seven days a week.

Side Trips:

If you load up on donuts and ice cream and need to walk it off, one of our favorite nature areas is just a couple miles away. The Pierce Cedar Creek Institute has all the easy walking trails you could ask for. This is a nature preserve that is also a "quiet place". No motors are allowed there. I don't think they even allow dogs. Note, you have to travel dirt and gravel roads to get there.

Just a bit west and south of Dowling is Hickory Corners. There you can visit the Gilmore Car Museum. It is huge, actually it is several buildings. There may even be a few antique cars puttering around the grounds.

Good Hart General Store

GOOD HART GENERAL STORE

The Trip:

Highway M-119 runs from Harbor Springs to Cross Village in the far northwest of the lower peninsula of Michigan. The road contains 137 curves as it winds along Lake Michigan and is known as the Tunnel of Trees. Some of these spots have a long history like the Old Council Tree and the Devil's Elbow. At the north end of the Tunnel of Trees is the famous Legs Inn. A well-known destination for biker's and lovers of Polish cuisine. There are a couple of lesser-known spots.

This road is a stunningly beautiful drive in all seasons. It is a particular favorite during summer and autumn. Since the whole thing is only about 20 miles it is a favorite day trip and many folks just roll along the whole way. Most any time and especially on the weekends, one place you don't want to miss is the Good Hart General Store. It is mid-way along the route and is easy to spot with its bright red paint and happy smiling people all about.

What you'll find:

The Good Hart General Store is one of those unusual places that everyone talks. It is quite small, but, don't let that fool you. On a weekend stop, you can easily be there for an hour or more.

The store serves as the Good Hart post office so it has become a meeting place for summer residents. It is a general store with supplies, groceries and locally produced jams and jellies. They have gifts and they have an fantastic deli serving up delicious meals. They also have the very best Pot Pies made anywhere in Michigan, if not the world. These pot pies are so good you may not want one from anywhere else ever again. That won't be a problem, they ship them anywhere and it is worth it.

On the weekends, just about anything can be happening here. Local farmers and artisans show up and set up shop outside of the store. There are picnic tables and people just seem to gather here and visit. On one Saturday some entertainers stopped in and decided to play for a while. With so much going on it is a great destination.

Directions:

From the Mackinac Bridge head south to Route 66 and go west to Cross Village. Take M-119 south about 10 miles to Good Hart.

From the south, make your way to Harbor Springs and head north on M-119 about the same distance. The store is in downtown Good Hart.

Side trips:

Just a bit north is a small sign pointing to the St. Ignatius Church. Originally established in 1741, the restored church is open for tours including a Native American burial ground.

South of the store is the Thorne Swift Nature Preserve. There is only a small sign to let you know this 30 acre natural wonderland is there. Three trails totaling 1 ¼ miles are well maintained and offer a nice stroll through the woodlands or down to a smooth stone-filled shore on Lake Michigan. The trails are comfortable and include boardwalks where necessary.

GORGEOUS GARDENS

The Trip:

Southern Exposure Herb Farm is just a short drive from Battle Creek, Michigan. The name doesn't tell the story very well. Yes there are herb gardens here, they are gorgeous, and beckon to you to wander through them, however, there is much, much more to this special place.

The short list of the activities here would be; specialty dining, amazing hands-on workshops, garden weddings and travel adventures. Add in spectacular gardens, beautiful pathways, gazebos and iron work and gourmet dining and catering, and you will begin to get the idea.

The owners are on site, everyone is friendly and welcoming. This is like a little bit of the old south that has been conjured up here in Michigan. Visitors are welcome to meander through the lush gardens and grapevine arbors and to pause and smell the flowers.

What You'll Find:

Special water features that attract birds, as well as

butterflies are all around. The gardens are packed full of herbs and flowers that are home to a variety of creatures. The farm facilities include restored farm buildings three of which are distinct and beautifully appointed dining rooms. Each dining area is unique.

The Hog House: Built on an 1840 farm site, Southern Exposure has completely renovated the farm's former structures into three lovely dining rooms with a Victorian flavor.

The Corn Crib: Renovated in 2000, the "Corn Crib" is home to a larger dining room with a covered patio area as well as a luxurious Bridal Suite designed to pamper the bride and her attendants on her special day.

The "Milking Parlour" is nestled on the ground level of our beautifully restored 1831 barn, which overlooks beautiful gardens and a fountain.

Dining here is an event. Each dining room is warmly decorated and very cozy in the latter part of the year. Meals are pre-fixe and the menu will follow a theme, usually southern in nature. During your meal the owners and the chef all make an appearance and speak with each table. I can only tell you that dinner here includes dishes not found anywhere around and the event is one heck of a show.

That isn't all. There are more than 40 work shops every year so folks can learn more about the delicious herbs grown here, and there are international tours.

This is one of those hidden gems that you will return to again and again. It is well worth the trip just to wander through the arbors and listen to the fountains.

Directions:

The farm is at 11269 N Drive North - From Battle Creek head up the Bellevue Road. Turn on 11 Mile and turn east again on N Drive North.
From Lansing take I-69 south to 15 1/2 Mile Road; head west.

Side Trips:

After seeing all of the great iron work and old farm architecture at Southern Exposure, you may want to decorate your own garden. On the east end of downtown Marshall you can find Keystone Antiques. Inside are architectural antiques from all over the country. There are columns, old archways, shutters, doors, iron work and a big selection of concrete statuary.

HARBOR LIGHT GALLERY

The Shop:

This one is definitely off the beaten path and definitely worth the trip. The shop features the work of Michigan artists with an emphasis on local attractions, such as the Port Sanilac lighthouse. The shop is attached to the Raymond House Bed and Breakfast in downtown Port Sanilac. If you don't know it is there, it is easy to drive right by as you tour U.S. 25.

Fans of fine photography will love this place. The work of Gary Bobofchak is available here. His photos of nature areas, waterfalls and woodland scenes are exquisite. He historic architecture photography captures the spirit of places like Williamsburg in such a way that you will feel like you are actually there.

Then you have the unique Broken China Jewelry designed and hand-crafted on site by Cristi Bobofchak. The pieces are created by using genuine heirloom china, breaking and polishing it and then, adding silver edging and details. The result is a full line of jewelry that is so unique it is even shown at fine art fairs. The gallery also offers frame art, pottery, and other crafts by local artisans. Almost everything is hand-made.

The Raymond House Bed and Breakfast is where you will find the gallery and it is easy to spot due to its distinctive architecture. The house was built in the 1820's by one of the town founders and was continuously occupied by the Raymond family for 112 years. In 1983 restoration work was begun. The original Victorian details have been preserved. The outside is adorned with a gingerbread facade, white icicle trim and the distinctive steep sloping roofs. Inside are the high ceilings, classic wood mouldings, framed ancestral photographs and hardwood floors. The entire inn is decorated with period furniture.

Directions:

Port Sanilac is on U.S. 25 on Lake Huron about halfway up the "thumb". An easy day trip of about two hours north of Detroit and about the same from Lansing. The Raymond House and the Harbor Light Gallery are just a couple of blocks south of the traffic light in downtown Port Sanilac, just 500 feet from Lake Huron.

Side Trips:

Just across the street is the Loop-Harrison Museum complex which includes the Loop Mansion, several historic buildings and one of the few operating Barn Theatre's left in Michigan.

Just outside the harbor at Port Sanilac is the Michigan Underwater Preserve. There are sixteen sunken vessels accessible to divers.

In nearby Croswell is a famous suspension bridge across the Black River. Only a block from downtown, the bridge is the site of the Swinging Bridge Festival every year. You will know it is the right bridge by the sign that reads, "Be Good To Your Mother-In-Law".

If lunch is in your plans, Just Joy's in Croswell may make the best BBQ in the state.

LAST ORIGINAL TOURIST TRAP

The Shop:

A little north of historic Castle Rock on the old Mackinac Trail, H-63, is Fort Algonquin, the last original, "up north Michigan" tourist trap. It looks like it, too.

The shop has the appearance of an old run down fort, is just north of St. Ignace, and is still a sort of trading post where you can find arts and crafts by local natives as well as a selection of "souvenirs" like those that were around in the 50's.

The old-timers will tell you that Chief Niwdoog, see below, not only founded the original trading post here, but also was the first to guide Europeans to Castle Rock.

What You'll Find:

It is easy to miss Fort Algonquin. It is so run down that it almost looks abandoned. There is a bit of flotsam and jetsam scattered around outside. All of this lends a bit of authenticity since the place looks like it just survived another ferocious upper peninsula winter.

Inside, the authenticity continues. The displays are disorganized and chaotic. The ceiling is literally festooned with all kinds of merchandise from dried herbs to dream catchers. Stuff is scattered everywhere You can find an arrow head, smoked fish or genuine elk antlers.

This is not a shiny, sparkling, modern shop. This is the way they used to do it when the only way to get to the upper peninsula from the lower was by taking the ferry. Take the kids, they won't see another one like this anywhere.

Directions:

From St. Ignace go north on the Mackinac Trail.

The Legend of Chief Niwdoog:

AN EARLY MISSTEP

Chief Niwdoog, while mostly forgotten today, may have played a pivotal, if blundering, role in early Michigan history. In fact, it is said that this remarkable Indian was even involved in the establishment of the country itself.

Chief Niwdoog was actually from the area now known as the Jersey Shore. Due to a major blunder he had to flee his home for the Canadian wilderness before finally arriving in Michigan.

It seems that he was part of a delegation that was sent to meet with the white men who were rapidly overrunning the island known today as Manhattan. Through a series of mistranslations and misunderstandings, Niwdoog traded Manhattan for some pop beads, instead of the property deeds to the rest of the continent, as he had been instructed to do.

A bit of haste and sloppy work and an island was sold for $24.00 and the continent was lost.

ON THE RUN

When the tribe heard about the trade, Niwdoog, was summoned to a Council of Elders to explain himself. The man may not have been a good trader but he wasn't a complete fool. Instead of going to the Council, he left his camp, said to have been where the Trump Towers stand now, and made his way across the Canadian border in the dead of night.

It may seem that Niwdoog was in a very bad spot but The Great Spirit was about to take an active part in his future. As Niwdoog made his way westward toward the great Huron Lake he happened upon a French encampment just as night was falling. While circling around to avoid the Europeans, he noticed a small stockade where a few Indians were being held prisoner. Among the prisoners was a young woman whose beauty was so great that it struck him even at a distance. Niwdoog decided immediately. He waited until the wee hours and with typical native stealth, crept in and helped all of the prisoners slip away into the forest.

The beautiful young woman was, in fact, a princess, Princess Ycnan, daughter of the chief. Niwdoog took her as his life mate and eventually became Chief Niwdoog when her father went to the happy hunting grounds in the sky.

FINDING CASTLE ROCK

Chief Niwdoog and his Princess continued on and eventually crossed the Sault Rapids into the Michigan wilderness. Stories of a tower of rock where one could hear the Great Spirit beckoned the Chief south where he and his tribe settled near what is now Castle Rock.

The legends say that Chief Niwdoog's descendants played a role in making peace with local tribes and helped preserve the pristine beauty of the local islands. It is also said that a descendant of the chief established the Pines Trading Post where the modern one stands today at the north end of St. Ignace.

LAVENDER LABYRINTH

The Trip:

Labyrinths are found around the world. They have been constructed since ancient times. There is a truly beautiful one right here in Michigan.

Unlike a maze, a labyrinth is a continuous circuit and you cannot get lost. Pilgrims entering the great cathedrals of France during the middle ages, walked the labyrinths inlaid in the cathedral floor to prepare them for the sacred experience they were about to participate in.

The Lavender Labyrinth is in the area of Oceana County known as Little Point Sable. World famous as a destination for sun and sand, this area is also home to rich farm lands and a long agricultural heritage. The Lavender Labyrinth is open to everyone and is in full bloom in July and August.

What You'll Find:

The labyrinth is on the grounds of Cherry Point Farm west of Hart and is a perfect place to walk amid lavender, rocks and wildflowers. The labyrinth, which takes about an hour to walk, is open to anyone: church groups, herb societies, drumming circles or individuals seeking new experiences. There is no charge, and reservations are not needed. Even if you don't have the hour, it is worth taking a look just to enjoy the sheer beauty of the labyrinth.

The farm includes a market that is famous for cherries, strudel and daily fish boils during the summer season. The address is 9600 West Buchanan Road, Shelby, MI 49455

Directions:

From Grand Rapids go north on U.S.21 to the Shelby exit head west.

The scenic route from either Pentwater or Montague is Route B-15.

Side Trips:

In nearby Hart, history buffs can enjoy one of the best Historic Districts in all of Michigan. There are several historic structures including an authentic blacksmith shop, log cabins, an antique fire barn and the Sackrider Church. The collections maintained by the district are unique as well. The Rider Indian Artifacts, thousands of pieces, hundreds of animated dolls and much, much more.

The Hart Montague Trail runs through the region. It is a multi use trail that offers access to agricultural areas that are otherwise inaccessible. A favorite of hikers and bicyclers, the trail makes for a full day trip all by itself.

In nearby Pentwater there are very unique shops like, Gardener's Folly and the Storybook Village, located in the picturesque downtown district.

MAGIC CAPITAL OF THE WORLD

The Trip:

Harry Blackstone became famous for his jaw-dropping magic performances. He was easily the most famous magician of his day and inspired many a spell-bound youth to learn the secrets of the magicians. In 1925, Magician Harry Blackstone moved to Colon. He and his brother Pete Bouton along with the stage crew would refurbish their illusion show during the summer months in preparation for their annual fall and winter tour throughout the United States. In 1927, Australian magician/ventriloquist Percy Abbott was invited to Colon by Blackstone. The two hit upon the idea of opening a magic manufacturing company - Blackstone Magic Company. However, it was short lived and the partnership lasted only 18 months.

What You'll Find:

Colon is a friendly community in south central Michigan. Downtown has a couple of fun shops and cafe's and, two very cool magic companies. Abbott Magic is on the west end of town. This is one of the oldest magic companies anywhere and they produce great magic tricks today. Fab Magic is on the east end of town and is also a big manufacturer of magic items. Both of these companies preserve the great traditions, manufacture magic paraphernalia and they both conduct live performances. In fact, magic is liable to break out anytime you enter one of these shops.

There is more. Every year for more than 75 years magicians from all over the world have held a gathering here. If you want to join in the fun, all you have to do is show up for the annual festival, Magic Week. There are often more than 1,000 magicians there.

Directions:

Colon is in St. Joseph County on Route 86 north of Sturgis.

Side Trips:

There are surprises and interesting destinations all around. Right on the edge of downtown colon are lakes that are known for the fantastic fishing. A dam on the river forms one of the lakes and that one is filled with stumps. All fishermen know what those stumps mean. A block away is an excellent bait and tackle shop.

The Museum - It isn't all magic in Colon. The town and area have a colorful history that is unique in all of Michigan. Just a block north of the main shopping district is an old church adorned with an enormous clock. When you find this you have found the museum. From the street it appears to be another, rather small, church building that has been converted to a museum. Looks can be an illusion like so many illusions in this community of magic. There is an addition that more than triples the original size that is hidden from view from the front. The church and the addition are filled with historical treasures.

The Eagles and the Hummingbirds - In the past couple of years there have been Bald Eagles nesting just outside of town. Ask any of the locals which road to take. The eagles are usually easy to see from the road. Hummingbird lovers should visit the River Lake Inn on Ralston Road. Extensive gardens surround the dining areas. Hummingbirds abound here.

The longest covered bridge in Michigan is just west of here on the road to Centerville. Just follow the signs to the Langley Bridge.

MOOSETALES GIFTS

The Trip:

Moosetales Gifts in Harrisville, Michigan may be the most unusual shop in all of northeast Michigan. Creative custom embroidery and rustic gifts may seem like an unusual combination. When nearly everything in the shop has a moose theme, the result is entirely unique.

When you first walk in, some folks are suprised at the friendly greeting. John and Judy are ready to assist with custom creations or to help you find the specialty items that may be on sale. Friendly service is just one of areas where this shop excels.

After that, you'll notice that there is an in-store rustic cabin decorated with rustic gifts and wild game pelts. Nearby is the gold fish pond with fountain and all around are hand-crafted items, many one of a kind and many made by local artisans.

What You'll Find:

In addition to Apparel - Books - Candles - Gifts - Treats & Sweets - there are some items you won't find anywhere else. How about moose themed shot glasses, hand made Grand Pa & Grandma Moose Dolls, camper lights made from shotgun shells, moose cookie cutters and a large collection of specialty signs.

Then of course there are the Lucy Moosy Specials. You have Lucy Moosey coffee, Lucy Moosey candy cups, delicious Lucy Moosey "Moose Toes" and Lucy Moosey "Moose Droppings".

Directions:

Harrisville is on Lake Huron at the junction of U.S. 23 and M-72 about 20 miles south of Ossineke. Moosetales Gifts is 1 block north of the light at that junction.

Side Trips:

Harrisville is a very small town but there are more side trips than you can take in a week. One of the most popular is the Quilt Block Trail. This is a driving tour through Alcona County that takes you to different locations where giant quilt blocks now adorn old barns.

Main street Harrisville is perfect for a stroll. You can get ice cream, visit the old Craftmaker's Cabin and shop in Harborplace Market. Just a few miles north of Moosetales is the Sturgeon Point Lighthouse. The lighthouse is open in summer and includes a gift shop. The old one room Bailey School House is also on the grounds of the lighthouse. Harrisville is also the site of Harmony Week, the second largest street arts and crafts fair in Michigan held every September.

MYSTERY IN ONTONAGON

The Story:

People have been mining iron and copper along the Ontonagon River since prehistoric times. All through the history of European trappers, settlers and miners entering the region, there have been discoveries of ancient mines. The copper from this region has a very specific content that is unique. Ontonagon copper has been found all along the Mississippi River, the Gulf of Mexico, the Caribbean and even in the Mediterranean region. These ancient miners sometimes left things behind.

In the late 1800's some locals were in the old Superior Mine near Rockland. They found an unusual object in the mine and brought it out as a curiosity. No one had ever seen anything like this before. It was about 12 inches long and about 1/2 inch in diameter. Really nothing more than a squared off rod. The main body was made of copper and one end had a band of iron wrapped around it lengthwise and riveted on.

Over time, as so often happens, interest waned and the unusual object forgotten. Eventually it was donated to the Historical Museum, cataloged and forgotten. Late last century a professor was visiting from Wisconsin and happened to spot the strange rod in a display case. He was amazed since, if his suspicions were correct, there was no reasonable explanation why this particular object should be in a Michigan mine. He convinced the Museum to loan the mystery object to his university for study. After careful research, including an opinion from a museum in Oslo, his theory was proven correct.

Vikings in Ontonagon?

Between 900 A.D. and 1,100 A.D. the Vikings were masters of the seas in their famous open ships. The over-lapping construction is familiar to all. It was unique to that period of time and was also unique because the construction technique, lap strake, involved riveting the planks to the ribs of the frame.

What You'll Find:

The tool rests in a display case in the Ontonagon Historical Museum in downtown Ontonagon. Visitors are welcome to handle it and examine the records. The museum is quite large and is filled with interesting items from the region including an enormous copper ingot.

Directions:

Ontonagon is on the shore of Lake Superior in the western end of the upper peninsula of Michigan about 15 miles from the Porcupine Mountains.

Side Trips:

Ontonagon is a great starting point for a number of adventures. The famous Lake of the Clouds is just a short drive away in the Porcupine Mountains. In Rockland is the very unique Henry's Never Inn where the best pasties anywhere are the special on Thursdays.

There are a couple of rather unusual shops to visit. The Rockland Depot houses an amazing spice vault with unusual spices and herbs from all over the world. In Ontonagon within site of the lighthouse across the river is the Gitche Gumee Landing. Inside you will find two remarkable shops. U.P. Candle Company produces and sells more than 40 fragrances of scented candles as well as hand-crafted jewelry. Also inside is Red Metal Minerals offering beautiful art and jewelry made from copper.

PORT ONEIDA

The Trip:

Port Oneida is one of the most unique historic districts in all of Michigan. Located within the borders of the Sleeping Bear National Lakeshore, it is one of the least visited attractions in the entire area. Perhaps that is because it doesn't appear on all Michigan maps. Empire is shown, as is Pyramid Point but, not Port Oneida.

Port Oneida grew into a sizeable community in the late 1800's as a result of the lumber industry and the work of Thomas Kelderhouse. Eventually the area included a dock on Lake Michigan, blacksmith shop, post office, general store and a boarding house.

When the trees were gone, the dock and mill were closed. By 1908, all of the buildings of the original town site, except the Kelderhouse residence, had been abandoned. A number of small farms struggled for existence. Most were no longer farmed after World War II.

When you enter the park, make a quick stop at the ranger station to pick up the Port Oneida booklet that has descriptions of the buildings and a simple map. You'll need the map to find you way around the district.

What You'll Find:

The trip to the Port Oneida Historic District can be enjoyed by car or bicycle. Note that some of these farms are on gravel roads. The tour meanders through the agricultural area of Pyramid Point and takes you to 10 - 15 farmsteads and the old Port Oneida schoolhouse.

The Charles Olsen Farm is one of the first stops you will come to. The office for Preserve Historic Sleeping Bear is located at this farm and, if open, is a good source for additional information. While you go from farm to farm you will also come across the Kelderhouse Cemetery and the farm next to it. The present house has also been used as a grocery store, telephone exchange and post office. Some of the barns are worth visiting like the Miller Barn. There is old machinery scattered around and some of the barns still have huge field stones as part of their foundations. The Bay View Hiking Trail also runs through the district and offers a convenient way to see some of the more remote parts of the district. Most of the buildings are well preserved and visitors are encouraged to wander around. Some, like the Weaver Farm, are badly weathered and in poor condition. It is not unusual to spend a couple of hours here and only see one or two other people. You can really enjoy the quiet and isolation of these beautiful farm lands.

Directions:

From Frankfort go north on M-22 through Empire and into the park.

From Traverse City go west on M-72 until you reach the park entrance at Empire.

Side Trips:

There are lots of things to do including a visit to the famous Sleeping Bear Sand Dunes. The Pierce Stocking Scenic Drive is a must visit when in the area. Spectacular vistas of Lake Michigan and gorgeous sunsets await. The covered bridge is one of the first treats you come to. Then there are about a dozen designated stops and short trails. If you take your time, you can find some incredible trees along with the dunes. Not far away is the Betsie Point Lighthouse and there are great shops in Empire, Beulah and Frankfort.

PURPLE PEAR

The Trip:

Alma, Michigan isn't usually mentioned when folks are discussing "must see" destinations. There is no warm sandy beach, no sunsets over a great lake and no famous island for a day trip. There is, however, a truly remarkable shop that is unlike any other anywhere in Michigan; the Purple Pear. Located in downtown Alma, the Purple Pear is known for gifts, home accents and gorgeous gift wrapping but, that is only part of the story.

What You'll Find:

As soon as you walk in you will know that you have found a different kind of shop. On the one hand is a display of Lilia, an Oprah favorite. There is a huge selection of jewelry and specialty shoes. Across the way is a charming general store department with custom coffee, gourmet treats and pure olive oil.

A bit further in is an entire department devoted to gifts for baby, wooden toys and cool clothes for kids, and every bit of it is of the very best quality. The Purple Pear thrives in the shadow of the big box stores that are nearby. They do it by offering difficult to find items, very high quality and an inventory that is made in Michigan or America whenever possible. The variety of merchandise categories is remarkable as well. In some cases this would just create chaos but not here. The owners have such a talent for display and presentation that it all works together. On top of that, the whole look changes seasonally. The shop will look completely different each time you stop in.

Finally, they make gift giving even more fun with their distinctive and complimentary gift wrapping.

Directions:

Alma is in the center of the state just off I-69 an hour north of Lansing. The Purple Pear is right downtown. Just look for the huge pear on the side of the building.

Side Trips:

Alma is the home of Alma College so one would expect a good coffee shop. You won't be disappointed. Edna Belles Coffee Shop is just down the street. In addition to coffee, she offers home made pies and candies.

Hometown Cellars Winery is located in downtown Ithaca, just a few miles south. They offer a wide variety of quality wines for visitors to sample. They also provide guidance in making your own wine. It is a very cool destination.

SHRINE OF THE PINES

The Trip:

The Shrine of the Pines is known as a "rustic furniture museum" It is certainly that but, there is more to the story. The museum sits in a small stand of pines on the famous Pere Marquette River and that setting is perfect for this timeless display of craftsmanship from another era. You can even watch the trout in the river from the museum observation deck. The contents of this Michigan treasure are the life work of Raymond W. Overholzer. Inside the log cabin that serves as the museum are over 200 pieces of his incredible rustic work.

What You'll Find:

This is the largest collection of rustic pine furniture in the world. The workmanship of this artisan is so fine that it is hard to think of these pieces as "rustic furniture". It is hard to believe that everything here is the work of one man. Mr. Overholzer collected and processed every piece of wood necessary for his masterpieces. These are more than just a table, beds, rocking chair and other furniture. Most pieces hold some secret hiding place that may not be obvious at first glance.

The large dining table was crafted from one white pine stump. It is more than 7 feet across and weighs in excess of 700 pounds. The finish on it, like most of the work here is drop dead gorgeous. The tour guide will probably show you some of the hidden compartments that are artistically concealed in the construction. The rocking chair is made mostly of roots. It too, is special. While it may look like other "rustic" rockers you have seen, this one is so well balanced that one push will set it to rocking and it will keep rocking more than 50 times. The stunning fireplace made of 70 tons of stone, there is a wooden gun rack with 39 wooden ball bearings and much more. The tour is well done and you can get a very good look at these and the other 200 works of rustic art.

Directions:

Located just south of downtown Baldwin, Michigan on route M-37.

Baldwin is about one hour north of Grand Rapids.

Side Trips:

One side trip that is a must do is right on the grounds of the museum. They have some tranquil trails running through the white pine forest. These woodlands paths are wheelchair accessible. The forest and the river attract wildlife and a wide variety of birds.

A few miles south is the Loda Wildflower Sanctuary. This is one of only a few wildflower sanctuaries located in a national forest. Note: some roads to the sanctuary are gravel

If you are in need of supplies or want an experienced river guide, stop at the M-37 Meat Market in Bitely. They can fix you up and they know where the fish are.

STORYBOOK VILLAGE

The Shop:

The Shop - Imagine a very special place ... where children can sail away in their imagination... Yes, there is such a place, without electronics or batteries, where exploration and creativity are encouraged through a unique gallery collection of award-winning books, art, storytelling treasures and gifts.

Storybook Village features a colorful cottage nook surrounded by cushioned window seats, a fish house with a secret passage to a cozy storybook theatre, and a sail boat complete with port holes for the children to peek out of and act out their own puppet shows and storybook productions.

This remarkable shop also includes puzzles, games, puppets, sing-along songs and story CDs', which encourages interactive play, listening, and memory skills. Handmade silk costumes (fairies, knights, capes and tutus) are also for sale, promoting creative and dramatic play.

There are colorful and playful books and gifts for early learners, books to encourage healthy choices and appreciation of the natural world, as well as traditional stories, classic anthologies, and whimsical tales from a variety of cultures, fueling the imagination and engaging book lovers of all ages.

One of the truly unique features is the story-telling. Every day the Storybook Village has story-telling sessions. Barb, the owner, gathers the children around and delights them with a story designed to fire their imaginations. Kids and grand parents alike love it.

What You'll Find:

The Storybook Village is one of the most unique shops anywhere in Michigan. The focus is entirely on children and their imaginations. Kids who go almost always want to go again. Adults delight in this place as well. Here is a shop that offers top quality items for kids that make perfect gifts. The shop is so unusual that it has even become a destination for folks who are sailing the Great Lakes.

When you stop in, make sure you check out the hand puppets. They are the coolest I have ever seen.

Directions:

Pentwater is on Lake Michigan and Pentwater Lake between Hart and Ludington.

Side Trips:

Shared Space Studio - This is another example of the creative spirit that flourishes in Pentwater. The Shared Space Studio, on the edge of town, houses arts and crafts studios and has a large multi-purpose community room where art classes, workshops and drop in and craft sessions are offered. They have a Visiting Artist program and walk-ins for all events are welcome. Just look for the colorful building that looks like it was quilted.

Bortell's Fisheries - This place is consistently voted the best fresh fish and seafood anywhere. You can get it fried or smoked or take it home and cook it up yourself.

There is no indoor seating but you can have your meal at the picnic tables outside. Bortell's is only open in the warm months so get it while you can. They are on S. Lakeshore Dr. up toward Ludington and have been for more than 30 years.

TASTY NUT SHOP

The Shop:

The Tasty Nut Shop has been serving up roasted nuts and delicious homemade candies since the middle 1920's. To get any real idea of how mouthwatering their fresh roasted nuts are, you only have to pause on the sidewalk outside and breathe in the incredible aroma wafting out of the store. The shop was originally the David Hotchin Drug Store. One of the owners asked an employee to roast some pecans and that was the beginning, those pecans were an instant hit.

A few of the exotic nuts available are: Natural Almonds from the Mid-East, Blanched Almonds from California, Jumbo Cashews from Mozambique and Pepitas from Mexico. Whatever you do, don't miss those Macadamias from Hawaii. These folks are just as well known for their pure chocolate candies. They carry milk chocolate, semi-sweet chocolate and sugarless chocolate. Every one of them is pure chocolate with no paraffin added.

Some of the candies include Raisin Clusters, Pecan Clusters and Jumbo Cashew Drops.

There are several more treats here but, you will have to make your way to White Pigeon, Michigan to try them out. These confections are so delicious, they have had orders from as far away as Belgium, Finland and New Zealand.

What You'll Find:

Today when you walk in the air is filled with the aroma of fresh baked chocolate and nuts roasted on the premises. Fresh roasted nuts are offered up in large glass jars. If you can make it past these goodies temptingly displayed up front, you can enjoy an ice cream or a soda at the 1950's style soda bar at the back of the store.

It is all decorated in Coca Cola colors. There are lots of collectibles and souvenirs on hand as well. Folks enjoy these specialties even if they have never stepped foot in the shop. The Tasty Nut House ships all over the world.

Directions:

White Pigeon, Michigan is on U.S. 12, the Great Sauk Trail that runs from Detroit to Chicago. The village is just north of Indiana and just east of

Route 131. When you arrive in town, ask anyone or just follow your nose to the Tasty Nut Shop.

Side Trips:

Down the street from the Tasty Nut Shop is the historic White Pigeon Land Office. It was the third to be opened in Michigan and is now operated as a museum by the St. Joseph County Historical Society. The museum is open on weekends.

Another great family business has been in operation nearby for years. Lowry's Books is an excellent independent book seller with shops in Three Rivers and Sturgis.

The Langley Covered Bridge is on the road to Mendon. It is the longest covered bridge in Michigan.

Mendon is home to two remarkable and historic structures. The Wakeman House is an old-fashioned lodging house on the original stage coach road. It is currently closed. Rawson's King Mill is just outside of town and is one of only a few remaining vertical shaft grist mills in America. It is in a beautiful county park.

TEN MILE CREEK FORGE

The Shop:

You will definitely leave the crowds behind when you visit this Irish/Celtic country gift shop. It is a beautiful drive and lovely setting.

A few miles outside Bark River, Michigan, is a very unusual shop. Ten Mile Creek Forge is described as a pottery and lighting gift shop. It actually holds original work by about 30 juried artists and is where George Potvin works his magic at the forge and blacksmith shop that is also on the grounds.

Artwork of local artists includes Irish crystal, jewelry, bath & beauty items, perfumes, colognes, hand-blown glass, stained glass, hand-made purses, raku, beautiful smoke-fire pottery , hand-carved scrimshaw, wood and soapstone carving, watercolor, photography, quilting, basketry, candles and more. That is just in the gift shop.

The Forge:

Specializing in hand-forged and completely hand-made knives and sheaths, George Potvin creates knives and scrimshaw work that is recognized world-wide. He hand-forges his blades and does all of his own heat-treating. He has created cable Damascus as well as traditional Damascus. Some knives are purposely primitive, while some are like polished jewels. They are always ready to use, to keep for your collection, or to give as gifts that will be treasured.

All knives come with hand-made sheaths that are designed, fitted and sewn to fit each individual knife. For handle material, choose from exotic woods from around the world, or indigenous birds eye or tiger maple. Hand Scrimshaw on indigeous deer antler is a favorite request.

George conducts one-on-one classes, teaching the fundamental techniques of blacksmithing from tending the forge, all the way to cutting, bending and finishing.

The Heart of La Branche:

While wandering between the gift shop and forge, you will notice lots of old machinery and tools. It is easy to miss a genuine oddity that these folks keep just outside the entrance to the forge. If you ask about the "Heart of La Branche" they will show you a very unusual stone. It is in the shape of a heart and is about the size of a 12 pack of soda. It is quite smooth, almost like a river rock, and if you whack it with a hammer it will make a sound like hitting an anvil. On top of all that, this small stone weighs over 240 lbs. and seems magnetic.

Several years ago a local group was mining gravel near the town of La Branche. Suddenly, the conveyor that moved the gravel came to a halt and, upon investigation, they discovered this most unusual stone jammed into the machine. After they cleared it out of the machine it was shown around and then forgotten. Later someone was going to sell it for scrap but the scrap yard called George Potvin and he came to the rescue. It really is an oddity.

Directions:

You can get to the Ten Mile Creek Forge by following the signs between Gladstone and Escanaba or go to Bark River and follow the signs.

Side Trips:

There is too much to see and do in this part of Michigan. One of my favorite places to eat is Solberg's Supper Club in downtown Felch. I still think they have the best filet in the upper peninsula.

At Jack's in Rapid River they make one of the best cinnamon roles you can find anywhere.

For a little culture, drive to downtown Escanaba and visit the East Ludington Art Gallery. These are local artists and the work here is plentiful and of very high quality.

THE TOMB OF THE COW

The Story:

Sometimes a rise to world fame has very humble beginnings; and so it was for Colantha Walker, the wonder cow.

The Northern Michigan Asylum opened in 1885 and eventually grew into a giant complex on the outskirts of Traverse City, Michigan. In fact, at one point the population of the hospital complex, 3,500, was greater than the population of the city at that time. The Asylum was self-sufficient with its own farms, gardens, fire department and power plant. It had its own orchards of peaches, apples and cherries, its own vineyards and vegetable gardens, field crops and a wide variety of livestock including a herd of cows. The most famous of these, actually the most famous inhabitant of the asylum period, was Colantha Walker, a grand champion milk cow.

In her long and storied career - from 1916 to 1932 - she produced 200,114 pounds of milk and 7,525 pounds of butterfat. In her best year, 1926, her annual production was a world record 22,918 pounds of milk. The official state average was

3,918 pounds.

When Colantha went to her reward in 1932, the staff and patients of the asylum held a banquet in her honor and erected a huge granite tombstone over her grave.

What You'll Find:

The Asylum closed in 1989 but the 500 acre property is being revitalized. The old asylum buildings are creamy brick and are architecturally spectacular. The complex is being transformed into an entire town with unique shops, galleries, restaurants, apartments and condominiums. Even if the tomb were not there, it is worth a visit just to see the gigantic structure that was once the asylum.

The Tomb of the Cow is tucked away on the south edge of the property near the old original barns. At a curve in the road just south of two champion Black Willows, the engraved stone sits between two trees. She is the only resident of the asylum to be buried on the grounds.

Colantha's accomplishments are commemorated by a Dairy Festival on the grounds each year.

Directions:

The Commons is just off U.S. 31. When you drive in, keep to the left to find the barns and the tomb.

Side Trips:

The Traverse City area is full of things to see and do and the entire Leelanau Peninsula can be explored.

If you are looking for the lesser-known, there is an original Adam's Fly on display just a few miles away in the Library in Kinglsey.

In Manton, just a bit further, is a foot locker from the Revolutionary War on display in the Veteran's Museum.

TREASURE IN CAPAC

The Story:

The original Kempf Model City was constructed in the early 1900's by Fred S. Kempf. He completed the work between the ages of 16 and 21. He made every single part by hand from scrap materials. The Mechanical Wonder was hailed as one of the most remarkable constructions of the time and was shown at events all over America. Then during a terrible train crash, the model city was destroyed. Fred Kempf and his wife lost their lives in that same train wreck in 1915.

Bruce and Irving Kempf began construction on a new model city that eventually was hailed as the "Mechanical Wonder of the Age". The Model City is a mechanical city built to the scale of 1/8 inch to the foot. It is 40 feet in length by 4 feet wide. The entire Model City is operated by a ½ horsepower motor found in the mountain at the end of the city. The city was fully operational and depicts a typical American city in the 1920's, although a few of the buildings were designed after specific buildings found in the United States. The mechanical wonder had more than 17,000 moving parts.

The city is fully populated with hand-carved people and has all the necessities of life. Cars that travel along the streets are serviced by a corner gasoline station. When they wear out, there is even a junkyard filled with tires and rusted iron.

For (19 years) it was displayed from coast to coast and throughout Canada: The Century of Progress, Chicago: Atlantic City's Steel Pier: Great Lakes Exposition, Cleveland: and Lakeside Park, Denver, Canadian National Exhibition and all the major State Fairs in the United States. During the Christmas seasons it was displayed in major department stores across the United States and many large movie lobbies from New York City to San Francisco. The Model City went into storage at the onset of WW II and was moved to Grand Blanc, Michigan. In 1988, the Capac Historical Museum purchased the mechanical wonder city.

What You'll Find:

Inside the Capac Historical Museum the "Mechanical Wonder of the Ages" is on display. It is being refurbished. The Model City is remarkable for its size and detail. When fully functioning it looks like an actual living city. Lights inside most of the structure reveal that life in "Model City" is not restricted to the streets. A man rocks comfortably in a chair inside the Maxwell Coffee House, and a new fire engine is poised inside the doors of the fire station."

Blue lights flash on and off at the welding factory indicating a night shift at work. A general store on the main drag displays bananas and other fresh fruit. All the more remarkable is the fact that the whole thing runs on small sewing machine motors and belts, no transistors and no computer chips. It is a great thing to preserve since I can't see how one could be built from scratch today.

The Rest of the Story:

The train wreck that destroyed the original mechanical wonder was described as "horrific" and the cars were quickly engulfed in flames. One of the last acts of the lives of Fred and Blanche Kempf was to literally throw their infant daughter out the window of the train. That act saved her life. In 1988, Bruce and Irving's niece, Hazel Kempf Mack; the little girl whose life was saved the day of the train crash that killed her parents, located the Model City in Grand Blanc and the events were set in motion that returned the city to its home in Capac.

The history, the photos and the "Mechanical Wonder of the Ages" are housed in Capac at the museum for all to enjoy.

TREASURE IN MANTON

The Trip:

Manton is a pretty little town up in Wexford County just a few miles east of Mesick. Mesick is home to that world famous Morel Mushroom Festival. Sportsmen and nature lovers may know of Manton because the area abounds with trails, parks, lakes and designated trout streams. The section of the Manistee River that flows just north is incredibly beautiful. Beautiful as all this is, there is another treasure in town, in fact, a couple of them.

What You'll Find:

The National Award Winning Veterans Museum was constructed and dedicated in 2002, the museum was entirely achieved by donations of material and labor. The Veteran's Memorial Museum Project was recognized as #1 in the nation by the Veteran's of Foreign Wars. Exhibits feature uniform displays, a military jeep, Japanese swords, a variety of weapons, Civil War items, and over 300 pictures of military personnel from the Civil War to Vietnam to Desert Storm. The most remarkable treasure you will find here is a trunk used by a soldier who served under

General George Washington during the revolutionary war. The Museum is owned by the City of Manton and the Museum Board. It is run and managed by volunteers.

Directions:

Manton is located at the crossroads of M-42 & Old U.S. 131

Side Trips:

Horse Shoe Bend - The Manistee River is just north of Manton, Michigan and provides some of the most pristine river scenes and experiences anywhere in Michigan. The Horseshoe Bend is a favorite destination on the river. This part of the river is a perfect choice for floating and kayaking. The river and trails wind through pines and hardwoods, wetlands and valleys. Every kind of northern Michigan wildlife abounds. When you get down to the dam, you can pause and watch the eagles fly.

A float trip will also bring you to two unique bridges: an arch timber bridge crossing Slagle Creek and a suspension bridge over the Manistee River linking the north end of the trail with the

Marilla segment of the North Country Trail on the west side of the river.

The Manton Pathway and Garden is a 1-1/2 mile nature walk. You will see everything from birds to small animals. There are bridges to cross and benches staggered along the trails. Manton Pathway and Gardens is open year round Monday- Sunday 8:00 a.m. to 8:00 p.m. and are located ¼ mile north of the US-131 and M-42 intersection, then west on Cedar St. next to the Dairy Bar.

TWO SHOPS AND A GHOST

The Trip:

The road trip involves making your way to Metamora, Michigan. This small town is rightly famous for the beautiful horse farms that surround it. In addition it is home to two remarkable shops and a "haunted inn".

ROADSIDE ATTRACTIONS!

When you see the crashed airplane at the side of the road, you will know that you are there. The shop sits well back from the road so the airplane crash helps. There are usually some unusual cars around and the front of the building is often decorated with one of a kind artifacts like giant dinos or original gas and oil signs. Don't let that fool you. Inside is a shop that is unique in every possible way. There just isn't anything like this in Michigan.

Upon entering, you might think you are in a museum. Antique maps are displayed near a 4 foot carved turtle. There may be an original Volkswagen Beetle or a restored Packard.

For people who are nuts about trains, this is the place with a selection that will appeal to model railroaders and rail line enthusiasts. The vast selection includes N-scale, HO, Lionel, Garden scale, Railroad crossings, signs, maps, engineer logs, vintage tickets, magazines, lanterns and more.

All over the store are antique and unique items, many that are one of a kind. At one time you could even get a stuffed hippopotamus head here. Their collection changes almost daily. If they don't have it, they can probably get it.

DESIGN WORKS

It is not everyday that you can visit the studio and workshop of a genuine artist but, that is exactly what Design Works Jewelry is in downtown Metamora.

This is where Zorka Pondell creates extraordinary jewelry. Zorka's love for horses is apparent in her designs. Highlighted in many equestrian publications, her artistry in producing beautiful equestrian pieces has brought her loyal fans throughout the United States & abroad. Her work is so exquisite that it has to be seen to be appreciated; words just won't do.

Her philosophy - "My objective as the designer is to create classic yet contemporary fine jewelry designs that are truly wearable. Each piece is treated as a work of art, with great attention given to each detail, guaranteeing the highest standards in workmanship from detailed hand carving of waxes, casting on to the final polish."

She fulfills these objectives over and over.

Directions:

Roadside Attractions is on Route 24 in Lapeer County. Downtown Metamora is a mile or so east. All of this is an hour north of Detroit.

Side Trips:

You won't have to go far. Just across the street from where Zorka performs her wizardry is the oldest restaurant in Michigan, the White Horse Inn.

In 1850, Lorenzo Hoard (1816-1888) purchased a

general store and transformed it into what today is, the White Horse Inn. He named it the Hoard House. He operated it as a boarding house charging 50 cents for overnight guests. The inn included a restaurant, general store and stagecoach stop until the stage service ended around 1910.

The age of this inn isn't the only thing that makes it unique. The upstairs is where you find Miss Lucy's Tea Room, Parlor and Gift Shop. This is also the area where "Lorenzo" the ghost is encountered most often. A pair of riding boots are always positioned at the top of the stairs. The story goes that Lorenzo slips these on in the dark of the night and wanders the village.

Lorenzo is often seen in the Tea Room or as a reflection in a mirror. Sometimes he just makes racket.

The downstairs is the restaurant dining room and tavern. The atmosphere is friendly and comfortable. At Christmas time, the inn offers horse-drawn sleigh rides around the beautifully lighted village.

NOTES:

NOTES:

NOTES:

NOTES: